An Invitation

to

Walk in the Light

Todd D. Bennett

Shema Yisrael Publications

An Invitation to Walk in the Light

First printing 2014
Second printing 2015

ISBN: 978-0-9768659-2-6

Printed in the United States of America.

Please visit our website for other titles:
www.shemayisrael.net

For information write:
Shema Yisrael Publications
123 Court Street
Herkimer, New York 13350

For information regarding publicity for author interviews call
(866) 866-2211

An Invitation

to

Walk in the Light

"But if we walk in the light as He is in the light, we have fellowship with one another, and the blood of Yahushua Messiah His Son cleanses us from all sin."
1 John 1:7

Table of Contents

I

In the Beginning

If you are holding this booklet in your hands then you have a choice to make. You can continue to read and possibly find yourself on a journey that transforms your life, or you may decide to stop reading and miss out on an incredible opportunity. While there are countless books available to read, not all can promise a life changing experience. That is a bold claim, but definitely true in this instance.

I grew up in a very typical small town in America. I was raised a Christian and regularly worshipped at a mainline Protestant denomination. While attending Sunday services I sang a variety of traditional hymns and one of my favorites was "Amazing Grace." There is one particular passage in that hymn that really strikes home . . . "I once was lost but now am found, was blind, but now I see."

While I sang that song as a youth, I believed that my eyes were in fact opened. I thought that I could see and had been fully exposed to truth. After all, I attended Sunday School. I asked Jesus into my heart as a young boy. I read my Bible and prayed every day.

Regardless, as I grew older I discovered that my church training had not fully prepared me for the questions that I found through my own reading of the Bible. I also was not equipped to answer some of the difficult questions posed by critics.

If I stayed within the protective bubble of my particular denomination and that limited sphere of people I could function without too much controversy. The problem was that some of the doctrines I had inherited did not seem to conform to the Scriptures that I was reading. At times, it appeared that the tough questions were avoided or swept to the side.

For instance, I was told that since I was a Christian, my Sabbath was on Sunday. Yet, when I read the Ten Commandments I found the following in my English Bible:

"*[8] Remember the Sabbath day, to keep it holy. [9] Six days you shall labor and do all your work, [10] but the seventh day is the Sabbath of the LORD your God. In it you shall do no work: you, nor your son, nor your daughter, nor your male servant, nor your female servant, nor your cattle, nor your stranger who is within your gates. [11] For in six days the LORD made the heavens and the earth, the sea, and all that is in them, and rested the seventh day. Therefore the LORD blessed the Sabbath day and hallowed it.*"[1]

So my Bible told me to "hallow" the Sabbath day and rest on the day that we call Saturday.[2] Regardless, my religion told me that this was something Jewish – not applicable to Christians. I always thought that Christians followed the Ten Commandments, but I was instructed that for a Christian to rest on this day constituted legalism. In fact, some went so far as to explain that every day is the Sabbath.[3]

This was taught despite the fact that the Sabbath was actually a sign that would demonstrate on a weekly basis whether a person was in a Covenant relationship with the Creator.[4] Since He rested on this day, all those in covenant with Him are supposed to follow His example and rest on the seventh day. This was not a day specifically for Jews.[5] The

---

[1] Exodus 20:8-11
[2] The word Saturday derives from "Saturn's day." It was the day set in honor of the Roman god Saturn, akin to the Greek god Cronus. It is part of the pagan calendar tradition that western culture has adopted and used for centuries.
[3] This is obviously a ridiculous concept with no support in the Scriptures. The Sabbath is specifically described as the seventh day of the week. It is also specifically a day of rest. Every day cannot be the seventh day and a day of rest. Otherwise, no one would be able to work. This is a simple example of the sloppy interpretation of Scriptures that are espoused throughout the various denominations of Christianity.
[4] Exodus 31:13-17
[5] The word "Jew" derives from the name Judah. It historically referred to those who descend from the Tribe of Judah or at some point joined with the Tribe of Judah. It also referenced a person who came from the region known as Judea. Currently, it applies to those who ascribe

Sabbath was set apart from the first week of creation when there were no Jews. It applied to all of creation from the beginning.[6]

I was therefore faced with quite a dilemma. Should I follow my religious tradition that directed me away from the 4th Commandment or should I actually obey the Commandment? The answer is obvious to me now, but when I was under the influence of false traditions it was quite perplexing. I definitely did not want to be "legalistic." I was taught that legalism was bad and any person who seeks to diligently obey the commandments is legalistic.

I now understand that to be an improper application of the term. Legalism has nothing to do with the proper observance of the Commandments, but rather the misuse or misinterpretation of the Commandments. It also applies to the adherence to the commandments of men over the Commandments found within the Scriptures.

Some people are legalistic when they erroneously believe that their obedience or "good works" justifies them. Clearly they are wrong. There is nothing we can do to to restore the relationship lost by man in the Garden of Eden. For that we need direct intervention from the Creator.

Incredibly though, the Creator promised great blessings to those who diligently heed His voice and carefully observe His Commandments.[7] In fact, one of the specific blessings attributed to diligent obedience was that He would heal all sickness and disease.[8] I found this particularly interesting since I was immersed in a Christian culture that was plagued with sickness and disease.[9] There seemed to be a

---

to the religion of Judaism or identify with the culture and progeny of the ancient Kingdom of Judah.

[6] The subject of the Sabbath is discussed in greater detail in the Walk in the Light series book entitled *The Sabbath.*

[7] Deuteronomy 28:1

[8] Exodus 15:26

[9] The so-called Christian nation of America is so plagued with disease and illness that the government is currently compelling all citizens to purchase health insurance so that they can be treated by the medical profession when they become ill. By doing this they are ignoring the root cause of the problem which is the fact that America is under a curse.

direct connection that the people were not experiencing this particular blessing because they were not diligently obeying the Commandments.

Imagine that! I grew up in a Christian denomination where I thought I was worshipping God, but I was actually taught not to obey Him because that was legalism. In fact, those who taught me this concept specifically stated that we cannot keep the Commandments because they were too difficult. If that were true, it meant everything I read about my God in the Old Testament was some sort of cruel experiment rendered upon the Israelites. Compelling the Israelites to obey something they could not, and then severely punishing them for their disobedience would render God sadistic and unjust. This certainly contradicted the "God is Love" mantra espoused in Christianity.

I later discovered that this entire scenario was inaccurate and untrue. God clearly loved the Israelites and that is why He gave them the Commandments that provided the path to blessing. Diligent obedience to those Commandments was their responsibility. Throughout the Scriptures obedience was always the hallmark for those who excelled when it was motivated by the love of God. By being directed away from the diligent obedience of the Commandments I was being robbed of the blessings promised to those who obey. So how on earth did things become so backward?

It all stems from the garden and the desire of the enemy to get mankind to disobey. The recent Christian paradigm actually traces back to an ancient heretic named Marcion from second century of the Common Era.[10] It was

---

[10] Marcion of Sinope lived between 85 CE and 160 CE. He was the Bishop of a heretical religious sect referred to as the Marcionites. He taught a dualist belief system that the god of the Old Testament was a separate and distinct god from the New Testament. As a result, he emphasized various texts over the Old Testament and essentially threw out the foundation of the faith. Because of the destructive nature of his false teachings, many attribute the decision to develop the canon of the New Testament to Marcion. The development of the canon of the New Testament was essentially an attempt to solidify orthodox doctrine and

later perpetuated through the centuries and has crept into most Christian thought. This construct developed largely because of the Christian teaching of "grace." Essentially, Christianity has labeled the Commandments as "the Law" and has juxtaposed "the Law" against "grace," as if these are two diametrically opposed concepts. Nothing could be further from the truth.

Popular Christian teaching has then misapplied the teachings of Paul by claiming that since we are "under grace," we are no longer "under the Law." This ill-fated logic results in the conclusion that we need to avoid the Law like a plague, lest we fall into legalism.

This leaves most people grappling with the Commandments, not knowing exactly what to do with them. They fail to recognize that the giving of the Commandments was an incredible act of grace because it revealed to mankind the conduct that pleased the Creator. This truth was supposed to be revealed by Israel to the nations of the Earth but they failed in their role as a nation of priests.

Since many teachers espouse the false belief that "we cannot obey the commandments" Christians by and large disregard them except for maybe the Ten Commandments. But there is the problem again, because the Sabbath is part of the Ten Commandments. It is the Fourth Commandment and the longest Commandment.[11] So what is a person to do?

Contrary to popular Christian teaching, we can keep the Commandments.[12] In fact, Moses specifically stated that

---

agree upon texts that supported that doctrine. Prior to that time, various letters and Gospels were circulating amongst the Assemblies, and were not treated as Scriptures.

[11] Exodus 20:8-11

[12] It is important to understand that a person is only expected to obey those commandments that apply to them. For instance, we can all endeavor to *love your neighbor as yourself.* Leviticus 19:18. We can control our sexual activities, our appetites and refrain from pagan practices. (Leviticus 18 - 20). We definitely can rest on the Sabbath. I dare say, an examination of the Torah clearly reveals that a person can certainly obey the Commandments. A common argument presented by those opposed to obeying the Commandments is the fact that there is no Temple. The existence or absence of a Temple never impacted the personal conduct prescribed in the Torah. If there is no Temple and no functioning priesthood, then you cannot obey the Commandments related to the Temple Service. The absence of the Temple is more a sign that Israel is under punishment. The

the Commandments were not too difficult.[13] What ultimately was too difficult, and considered to be a burden, were the numerous man-made rules and regulations added to the Commandments through the traditions of men.

This was one of the very specific things that the Messiah addressed as He confronted the religious leaders of the Jews.[14] It was also referred to by Peter when he addressed the Jerusalem council concerning the traditions imposed by the Pharisees. He called them a yoke on the neck *"which neither our fathers nor we are able to bear."*[15]

When the Scriptures refered to the burden of legalism they were dealing with situations when men treated traditions as equal to or superseding the Commandments of the Creator. So throughout much of my life I was essentially told a lie and then instructed to disobey the Commandments of the very God I was supposed to be serving. Amazingly, that was not all. I had inherited many other false teachings and traditions. Ultimately I realized that the very things the Messiah had warned and taught against had crept into my own religion.

This placed me in a very precarious position with my Creator Who I really did not even know. As it turns out, through many of my actions and beliefs I was actually worshipping a counterfeit god. I was being set up for failure and destruction by my religion. My religion did not even teach me the Name of the God I worshipped. In fact, I

Messiah came in the Order of the Melchizedek Priesthood and offered the needed sacrifice to restore mankind through the Renewed Covenant. Once we recognize that we are covered by the Blood of the Lamb as prophetically revealed through the Passover, we can then enter on the Covenant path through the Renewed Covenant mediated by the Lamb of God – the Messiah.

[13] Deuteronomy 30:11

[14] When the Messiah was confronted regarding why His disciples did not follow the traditions of the elders He responded as follows: "[6] *He answered and said to them, "Well did Isaiah prophesy of you hypocrites, as it is written: This people honors Me with their lips, but their heart is far from Me. [7] And in vain they worship Me, teaching as doctrines the commandments of men. [8] For laying aside the commandment of God, you hold the tradition of men - the washing of pitchers and cups, and many other such things you do. [9] He said to them, All too well you reject the Commandment of God, that you may keep your tradition."* Mark 7:6-9. See also Matthew 15:1-9.

[15] Acts 15:10

discovered that it intentionally hid the Name from me.

There is an interesting riddle found in the Scriptures as follows: "*Who has ascended into heaven, or descended? Who has gathered the wind in His fists? Who has bound the waters in a garment? Who has established all the ends of the earth? What is His Name, and what is His Son's Name, if you know?*" Proverbs 30:4.

My lifetime of religious attendance had not taught me the answer to this very basic riddle. I did not even know the Name of the Father and the Son – the Ones Who I relied upon for salvation. Now, I was taught that the Name of the Father was Jehovah and the Name of the Son was Jesus, but these Names are non-existent in the Hebrew language. In fact, they are fabricated English names that have only been in use for around 500 years. I truly had inherited lies since both the Father and the Son had revealed their Names in the Hebrew language – not English.

When I understood this, I realized that I was actually experiencing a fulfillment of prophecy. In my English Bible the Prophet Jeremiah provided: "*[19] O LORD, my strength and my fortress, my refuge in the day of affliction, the Gentiles shall come to You from the ends of the earth and say, 'Surely our fathers have inherited lies, worthlessness and unprofitable things. [20] Will a man make gods for himself, which are not gods? [21] Therefore behold, I will this once cause them to know, I will cause them to know My hand and My might; and they shall know that My name is the LORD.*" Jeremiah 16:19-21.

This prophecy was clearly speaking to me and most Christians for that matter. We have been making gods for ourselves that are not gods. We have been applying fictitious names and incorrect teachings to the Father and His Son.

Notice the last passage that promised that the Gentiles, also known as the Nations, would know that the Name of the Creator is "the LORD." Despite the fact that I had been calling Him "the LORD" all of my life, it is obvious that "the LORD" is not a name. Rather, it is a title that the

English translators use to replace the Hebrew Name of the Creator.

I later discovered that there were answers to my questions hidden beneath the English translation. Indeed, the Name of the Creator is depicted in the modern Hebrew as יהוה and the Ancient Script as 𐤉𐤄𐤅𐤄. The Hebrew language consists of 22 characters, originally written as pictographs. Each pictograph has a meaning and by combining them together they form words with meanings.

The ancient message has been lost or diluted through time and translations. Just as the ancient messages provided through the constellations as signs in the heavens have been misrepresented so have the ancient words.[16] Most people who read a translation of the Bible are unaware of the rich content contained in the original language. They also fail to understand that translators have fallen short in completely transmitting the contents of the original texts primarily because of language differences.[17]

For instance, the English and Hebrew languages read in the opposite directions. While English reads from left to right, the Hebrew reads from right to left. This simple difference actually has profound effects on the cultures and the thought processes of those who communicate in these

---

[16] The Scriptures describe the stars and the planets as signs. (Genesis 1:14). Indeed, the constellations, known as the mazzaroth in Hebrew, are intended to read like a scroll in the heavens. Prior to entering into Covenant, Abram was told to look up and "count" the stars. (Genesis 15:5). The word for "count" is "sepher" in Hebrew. It literally means: "scroll." From this we are given the image that the stars and the constellations are unrolled like a scroll in the heavens that can be read and understood. They tell a story for all of the inhabitants of the earth to read and understand. Sadly, most have failed to understand this ancient message provided for by the Creator, and most Christians have relegated the mazzaroth to pagan astrology. Sadly, astrology has adulterated the original messages of the Creator that have been lost. The point is not to ignore the signs, but to discern their original meaning.

[17] This statement in not intended to be a knock against translators. All of us who were not raised in the Hebrew language and culture owe a great debt of gratitude for translators who have made the texts readable to those of other languages. The point is to recognize their limitations and attempt to discern when the translations fall short. This may be a difficult truth for someone raised on a particular English translation believing that it is the "inerrant Word of God." This subject is discussed in greater detail in the Walk in the Light series book entitled The Scriptures.

"opposite" languages.[18]

The Hebrew language consists of consonants. The vowel sounds are generally not represented by characters in the original text. The common pronunciations of the Name of the Creator are Yahuwah or Yehowah,[19] and the Name is often represented in English by the consonants YHWH.[20] Since the pronunciation is a disputed issue the Name will be presented as YHWH through the remainder of this book.

This Name was hidden from me my entire life just beneath the translation of my English Bible. Indeed, due to these translation traditions, the Name is hidden from almost the entire world. Even Jews, who maintain their Scriptures in the modern Hebrew language, do not speak the Name and actually replace the Name with the title "Adonai" or "Hashem."

These traditions go against the entire thrust of the Scriptures that describe the revelation of YHWH and His Name to all of the earth.

This is no small issue. YHWH revealed Himself with a unique Name in a specific language. He desires for that Name to be known and we are either part of the problem or part of the solution. In fact, the first words spoken by YHWH at Mount Sinai were: *"I am YHWH your Elohim . . ."* This was the first Commandment of the Ten Commandments – not an issue to take lightly. Notice that

---

[18] See *Hebrew Thought Compared to Greek*, Thorleif Boman, W. W. Norton & Company (1970).

[19] There are also those who transliterate the Name as Yahweh and pronounce it as Yah-way. Although probably the most common and popular usage, it does not appear to be a consistent pronunciation when we consider how the Name is pronounced when imbedded in other names. For instance, the Hebrew name Matthew is pronounced Mattityahu. It means: "gift from YHWH." The "yahu" portion is intended to reference the "YHW" portion of the Name. We see this throughout the Hebrew language and therefore it seems best to be consistent with this pronounciation when the Name stands alone. This subject is discussed in greater detail in the Walk in the Light series book entitled *Names*.

[20] It is important to remember that the Hebrew language reads from right to left. When providing the Name as English consonants it reads from left to right. This is only done to aid the reader in recognizing and pronouncing the Name. It is not intended to replace the Hebrew Name that always reads from right to left.

YHWH refers to Himself as Elohim – not God.[21]

His Name is so important that in the Third Commandment He provides: *"You shall not take the Name of YHWH your Elohim in vain, for YHWH will not hold him guiltless who takes His name in vain."* Exodus 20:7. The word translated as "vain" in English is "shaw" (𐤀𐤅𐤔) in Hebrew. It means: "desolate or destroy." Therefore, the purpose of the Commandment is so that the Name of YHWH would not become "naught," which is exactly what has happened through the texts and the religions that are supposed to represent Him.[22]

---

[21] The word God is an English word with teutonic origins. It has been used to refer to pagan gods and the better word to use when referring to YHWH is Elohim. This subject is discussed further in the Walk in the Light series book entitled *Names*.

[22] When confronted with this truth many religious individuals ignore it and choose instead to follow their own tradition. This is a serious mistake and reveals the heart of the individual. They call those who desire to properly exalt the Name as "legalistic" and indicate that this is not an important issue. Nothing could be further from the truth. Someday we will all stand before Him and give an account for what we did with His Name. There is actually a special Scroll of remembrance that was written *"for those who fear YHWH and meditate on His Name."* Malachi 3:16.

2

Time

Once we are confronted with truth that conflicts with our traditions and beliefs, we have a choice to make. This is more difficult for some than it is for others. I always had a feeling that there was more than I was being told. As a result, it was not hard for me to discard the lies and grab ahold of truth when it was revealed. Others struggle to maintain the status quo, or what they consider to be normal. Change is not comfortable and it is usually avoided by most.

People develop their paradigms at a very young age. In fact, at the beginning of a person's life, in their mother's womb, they are learning.[23] After their birth, the learning accelerates. What began as a simple existence within the safety and protection of their mother's body expands incredibly in size and scope.

Life suddenly includes a home, other family members and maybe even a pet. The sights, sounds, tastes and external stimulation all combine to form and shape the child's existence. A worldview begins to develop from their unique life experiences, surroundings and perceptions. Since their personal lives are generally more limited during their younger years, much of the information that they use to develop their worldview is taught to them within that closed environment.

For instance, in years past, a child's religious training would primarily occur in the home and in church. Children were typically taught about God from their parents and also from Sunday school teachers. Now, with the advent of technology, children receive an enormous amount of

---

[23] See article entitled *Babies can learn their first lullabies in the womb*, October 30, 2013 from study at University of Helsinki, www.sciencedaily.com.

information from additional sources including television and the internet. At the same time, the number of American children attending Church or Sunday school is decreasing rapidly. Of those children who still attend church, many are receiving a diluted message filled with false traditions and even outright lies.

So those paradigms and the information used to formulate them are now very different than in the past. As a result, we see many children being raised who know very little about the Bible, save some traditional myths that circulate through society.

For instance, they might have heard about Noah's ark and the great flood, but chances are they could not tell you why YHWH was compelled to destroy certain life forms. Particularly, they would probably be oblivious to the genetic corruption that had occurred on the planet due to the actions of certain fallen angels.[24]

They were never provided with this information because they either gained their understanding from an inaccurate Hollywood movie or because those who taught them failed to understand what happened at the beginning of this present existence. Another fact that they might claim to know is that all of the animals went onto the Ark two by two. Sadly, that is not accurate. While there were two of every unclean animal, there were actually seven pairs of every clean animal.[25] This is a fact clearly provided in the Scriptural text but often ignored or neglected.

The reason that this fact is not recognized or taught by most is because their religion or tradition is probably not concerned about such distinctions. That is part of the problem that faces modern religions and modern man. The

---

[24] Genesis 6:3-4, 11-12. There are certain non-canonized texts, such as 1 Enoch and The Book of Giants that provide additional information concerning these fallen angels, also known as Watchers. While these texts are not included within the canon of Scripture they were both found among the Dead Sea Scroll that supports their use, at the very least, as supplemental teaching texts.
[25] Genesis 7:2-4

Creator is very concerned about distinctions. He cares about how you act and how you live. He even cares about what you eat.[26] The reason that He cares about these things is because He created man "In His Image."[27] He designed mankind to be "holy" as He is "holy."[28] The word "holy" is actually "qadosh" in Hebrew and it means: "set apart." Therefore, mankind is supposed to be "set apart" from the rest of Creation.

Because of this incredible privilege, man is special – different from all other created beings. Man is not an animal, and is not supposed to act like an animal. Therefore he is expected to live according to certain guidelines established for those beings made in the image of the Creator of the Universe. He holds a position of honor in Creation and was intended to be a co-worker with the Creator in establishing His Kingdom on Earth.

Herein lies the dilemma facing mankind. Will he live according to his purpose and function in his designated role or will he do what he wants to do? This has been the problem plaguing man from the beginning of time. He refuses to live a holy (set apart) existence, which is defined by obeying the Commandments. Therefore, he is precluded from dwelling with the Creator. Instead of obeying the Commandments which leads to blessings and life, he chooses to disobey which leads to curses and death.

We can discern from the very first Hebrew character in the Scriptures that the focus of Creation is to fill a house through a Covenant. The Scriptures start with the word "Beresheet" which looks like this in Ancient Hebrew

---

[26] The Scriptures actually define what is food fit for consumption. The Creator made man and He also designed certain animals with specific functions. Some are designed to be eaten, while others are not intended for consumption. These instructions are meant to bless mankind by informing us what to eat and what not to eat. Obedience to the instructions results in our being blessed with good health while disobedience leads to sickness and disease. It is critical to realize that the Commandments are for our good. Those instructions are discussed further in the Walk in the Light series book entitled *Kosher*.

[27] Genesis 1:26-27

[28] Leviticus 19:2

𐤈𐤉𐤔𐤀𐤓𐤁. The Hebrew language reads from right to left and we will be looking at the Ancient Hebrew because it is more authentic than what is commonly referred to as Modern Hebrew.[29]

The Hebrew word "Beresheet" (𐤈𐤉𐤔𐤀𐤓𐤁) literally means: "in beginning." Amazingly, in the Hebrew text we see an enlarged "bet" (𐤁) as the first letter or "pictograph." So in the original language, we would see something like this:[30]

$$𐤈𐤉𐤔𐤀𐤓𐤁$$

Remember that each pictograph has a meaning and the meaning of the Hebrew letter "bet" (𐤁) is "house." With the emphasis on the "bet" we see the focus placed on a house. In fact, this first word contains the Hebrew word for "house" which is "beit" (𐤕𐤉𐤁). The first word also includes the word for Covenant, which is "brit" (𐤕𐤉𐤓𐤁) in Hebrew.

The astute observer might also note that the Covenant (𐤕𐤉𐤓𐤁) surrounds the word "esh" (𐤔𐤀) which means: "fire." So there are profound messages contained in the first word of the Scriptures that are only discernable in the

---

[29] The Hebrew language is a very ancient language, believed by many to be the original language of Creation. What we currently see as "Modern Hebrew" is not the original Hebrew script. Modern Hebrew is actually a language believed to have resulted from the Babylonian exile of the House of Judah. It does not represent the script used by the Israelites before the division of the Kingdom of Israel into two houses after the death of King Solomon. After the death of King Solomon the Kingdom was divided between the northern tribes, known as the House of Israel and the southern tribes, known as the House of Judah. Each of these houses resulted in a unique kingdom with a unique prophetic history. The restoration and reuniting of the divided kingdom is actually the context and culmination of history. While the House of Judah remained intact as an identifiable people group known as the "Jews," the House of Israel completely lost their identity and relationship with YHWH as prophesied by the prophet Hosea. (see Hosea 1:1-11). That is why the Messiah came for "the lost sheep of the House of Israel." Matthew 15:24. He came to unite the two houses and restore the Kingdom of Israel. (see Ezekiel 37).
[30] The ancient Hebrew font used in this text is better known as paleo Hebrew. It is a font created by the author to represent the original pictographs based upon archaeological findings. Just as each individual has their own particular writing style, so these fonts depict the different "styles" of the individuals who wrote these pictographs that have been preserved through time and discovered through archaeology.

Hebrew text. One can only imagine all of the treasures waiting to be discovered within the Hebrew Scriptures.

Clearly, the message involves filling a house through a covenant. Now when we proceed past this first word to the story of Creation, we can discern that the planet was being restored after judgment and destruction.[31]

This is what many fail to realize. The first sentence in an English Bible declares: *"In the beginning God created the heavens and the earth."* Genesis 1:1. While there are 10 English words in that statement, there are actually only 7 Hebrew words and one special word is not even translated.

Here is what we see in the ancient Hebrew script:

ﬧﬡﬠﬡ ﬨﬠﬧ ﬩﬩ﬧﬡ ﬨﬠ ﬩﬩ﬡﬥﬠ ﬠﬧﬡ ﬨ﬩ﬥﬠﬧﬡ

We just mentioned the existence of the enlarged "bet" (ﬡ). It is the first message contained in the written Scriptures, and it can only be seen in the Hebrew. Couched within the seven words in the Hebrew text there are two occasions when we see a mysterious word pronounced "et."

The word contains an "aleph" (ﬠ) which is the first letter in the Hebrew alphabet. It also includes a "taw" (ﬨ), which is the last letter in the Hebrew alphabet. The word

---

[31] Creation appears to begin as a dark and ominous event, and many speculate why things were in such a state. The Messiah made a very interesting statement regarding His second coming. He stated that He would come and divide the sheep from the goats and He would tell the sheep: *"inherit the kingdom prepared for you from the foundation of the world (katabole)."* Matthew 25:34. So He was speaking of a kingdom being prepared from the foundation of the world. When we read about the time "before the foundation of the world" – "katabole" (καταβολῆς), we see something very interesting. The Greek word "katabole" (καταβολῆς) actually means: "destruction, a casting down, break down or disintegration." So it appears that there was an existence that occurred before the "casting down or destruction." This explains the New Testament text of 1 Peter 1:20 which indicates that the Messiah *"was foreordained before the 'foundation of the world' (καταβολῆς), but was manifest in these last times for you."* It also explains the idea of predestination as described in the text of Ephesians 1:4. *"Just as He chose us in Him before the 'foundation of the world' (καταβολῆς), that we should be set apart and without blame before Him in love."* So things happened, decisions were made, and destinies were determined before the destruction which leads us to understand that there was a destruction prior to the creation that we read about in Genesis 1:3. Since that creation, including our present understanding of time, a kingdom is being prepared – a house for a Covenant people.

looks like this "את" in the Modern Hebrew and this "𐤀𐤕" in the more ancient Hebrew script.[32]

We can see from the ancient text that the "aleph" (𐤀) represents the head of an ox and signifies strength. That strength is bridled and directed so that ground can be prepared to receive seed and produce fruit. The ox is, therefore, appropriately placed in the first position, and reveals the message of the entire alphabet or rather "aleph bet."[33]

The "taw" (𐤕) represents a "mark" or "signature" and it means: "covenant." As the final character in the 22 letter alephbet, we can see that the entire progression leads to a covenant. This is the story contained within the Hebrew alephbet. As a result, the mysterious Aleph Taw (𐤀𐤕) that is woven throughout the Hebrew text also contains an important message. Since it contains all the letters of the Hebrew language it also encompasses the words of the Hebrew language. Creation was spoken into existence. Therefore, the Aleph Taw (𐤀𐤕) represents the essence of Creation.

There is an incredible message associated with the Aleph Taw (𐤀𐤕) and it can only be seen in the Hebrew language. It is never translated so it is rarely discerned by someone who exclusively reads a translation. This is something important to recognize, because translations are missing some vital information that can only be found in the

---

[32] This is "the Word" described in the New Testament Gospel of John. "[1] *In the beginning was the Word, and the Word was with God, and the Word was God.* [2] *He was in the beginning with God.* [3] *All things were made through Him, and without Him nothing was made that was made.*" John 1:1-3.

[33] We commonly refer to our English character set as the "alphabet" because letters "alpha" and "beta" are the first two letters of the Greek alphabet. The Hebrew language is much older than the Greek language, and is the very source language from which everything was created. See *The Origin of Speeches Intelligent Design in Language*, Isaac E. Mozeson, Lightcatcher Books, 2006. The first two characters in Hebrew are "aleph" (𐤀) and "bet" (𐤁). So we can see that the Hebrew language is the origination of the term "alphabet" so when referring to the Hebrew character set it is better to refer to the "alephbet."

original Hebrew language.[34] The Aleph Taw (𐤗𐤀) is only one example of this problem. If you are a truth seeker then you must move beyond a simple translation.

Now continuing with the creation account, the text then goes on to declare: *"The earth was without form, and void; and darkness was on the face of the deep. And the Spirit of Elohim was hovering over the face of the waters."* Genesis 1:2.

This description in verse 2 is not a beautiful paradise but rather a creation described as empty with extreme darkness covering the abyss (the deep). In the Hebrew, the word translated as "without form" is "tohu" (𐤅𐤄𐤀). It means: "empty, confusion, uninhabited." This was not the original condition of the planet. The Prophet Isaiah clearly provided that YHWH did not create the earth "tohu."[35] So while the original creation was described in Genesis 1:1, something happened between that time and the condition of the planet in Genesis 1:2.

The Spirit was hovering over the abyss as the Creator was in the process of restoring creation or recreating. That restoration began on Day 1, but Day 1 started at Genesis 1:3-5 when Elohim said: *"let there be light."* Now this blows the minds of many who were taught to believe that Genesis 1:1 describes Day 1.

This is because most people reading English translations are reading an ancient eastern text from a western mindset and perspective. An eastern language and mind views time as cyclical while western individuals view time as linear. This difference in language and thinking tends to be the primary disconnect that many in western Christianity suffer from. You cannot simply read these ancient texts through a modern lens. You must look back and interpret the texts from within the context that they were written.

---

[34] The subject of translation issues is discussed in the Walk in the Light series entitled *The Scriptures.*
[35] Isaiah 45:18

What modern Christianity has done is quite the opposite. It has adapted these ancient teachings to fit within a modern industrialized culture focused on individual liberties, consumer capitalism, prosperity, wealth accumulation, the pursuit of happiness, personal achievement and entertainment. These are not necessarily the focus of ancient cultures and those ancient texts.

Therefore, modern Christianity in many ways contains a diluted and distorted message, juxtaposed against the one contained within the Scriptures. That disconnect is perpetuated by the labeling of the texts contained in Christian Bibles. The Hebrew texts are collectively referred to as "old" while the Greek texts are collectively referred to as "new." As a result, the ancient Hebrew texts are often neglected or relegated as secondary to the "newer" Greek texts.[36]

This realignment of texts is like building a house on sand. It will not produce the desired result, only destruction.[37] The Hebrew texts referred to as the Old Testament are the foundation upon which the Covenant House is built. In fact, in the days of the Messiah, and well after His death, resurrection and ascension, the Hebrew Scriptures were the only Scriptures in existence.[38] In fact, it was centuries later and the Christian religion developed that the New testament was compiled.

The disconnect from the original faith contained in those Hebrew Scriptures is not immediately apparent due to the translations used by western Christians. This is a very precarious situation for those who exist in the Christian religious construct.

The Creator chose an eastern language, namely

---

[36] Most Greek texts used in the New Testament are copies of autographs that date back almost 2,000 years so they certainly cannot be deemed "new."
[37] See Matthew 7:26-27
[38] Numerous references in the New Testament refer to "The Law and the Prophets" which were the Scriptures of Yisrael at the time. See Matthew 5:17, Matthew 7:12, Matthew 22:40, Luke 16:16, Acts 13:15 and Romans 3:21. For a more detailed discussion of the texts that constituted The Scriptures see the Walk in the Light series book entitled *The Scriptures.*

Hebrew. He also chose to reveal Himself through eastern cultures. Therefore, that is the framework within which we must view and interpret the Scriptures. An important part of that framework involves time.

Those seven Hebrew words previously referred to in the beginning of the Scriptures contain many mysteries, and they also reveal an emphasis on the number seven. In fact, the Scriptures proceed to describe the creation, or recreation, within a seven day period. On Day 1 when Elohim said: *"Let there be light"* He was not referring to the sun. That was created on Day 4.[39]

The Light of Day 1 was different from the sun. It was not necessarily the Creation of light itself, but rather the manifestation of light into the physical realm. The Hebrew text actually states: *"exist light."* Light overcame the intense darkness and when read in the Hebrew we are told that Elohim saw that "ᕁᕁ-the light" was good. In the Hebrew text, the mysterious Aleph Taw (ᕁᕁ) is affixed to "the light." Of course, the New Testament indicates that this "light" was also the Word.

The mystery of the Hebrew passage is actually explained in the New Testament writing called the Gospel of John. *"1 In the beginning was the Word, and the Word was with Elohim, and the Word was Elohim. 2 He was in the beginning with Elohim. 3 All things were made through Him, and without Him nothing was made that was made. 4 In Him was life, and the life was the light of men. 5 And the light shines in the darkness, and the darkness did not comprehend it."* John 1:1-5.

So the text is explaining a mystery that was not fully understood until the Messiah came and explained that He was the Aleph Taw (ᕁᕁ) – the Word that was from the beginning.[40] That Word was the light that was manifested into Creation.

This makes perfect sense when we read that the sun

---

[39] Genesis 1:16
[40] Revelation 1:8, 1:11, 21:6, 22:13

was later created on Day 4. Here is what a typical English translation provides: *"Then God said, Let there be lights in the firmament of the heavens to divide the day from the night; and let them be for signs and seasons, and for days and years."* Beresheet 1:14.

There is a mystery in this text that can only be fully understood in the Hebrew. The Hebrew word translated as "seasons" is "moadim" (𐤌𐤏𐤃𐤅𐤌). The word "moadim" does not mean "seasons" but rather "appointed times." The Appointed Times are special appointments established by YHWH.[41] The Sabbath is a weekly Appointed Time that occurs every seventh day. There are also seven annual Appointed Times that occur throughout the year. The emphasis on seven cannot be ignored as the framework for time in this creation. This is a pattern revealed through the first seven words of the Scriptures.[42]

The Appointed Times are described in the Scriptures known as the Torah.[43] They are often characterized as "Jewish Holidays" which is absolutely incorrect. The Scriptures specifically describe them as belonging to YHWH.[44]

They are specific times that YHWH schedules to meet with His Covenant people and He uses them to fulfill His Covenant plan. Anyone who is in a relationship with Him should be aware of these times and should be keeping these appointments.

---

[41] The moadim are discussed in detail in the Walk in the Light series book entitled *Appointed Times*.

[42] The subject of time as revealed through the Scriptures is discussed in the Walk in the Light series books entitled Appointed Times and The Final Shofar.

[43] The Torah, often called "The Law" by Christians, is also called the Pentateuch or the 5 Books of Moses. It is better referred to as "instructions" because the Torah provides the righteous instructions of YHWH that reveal the way to blessings and life. It also describes the punishment and curses associated with disobedience that leads to death. It was a gift provided by YHWH to reveal how He operates His universe. It was meant to teach people the way of righteousness (Exodus 24:12). The people then had to choose blessings or curses, life or death. (Deuteronomy 30:19). The Torah is discussed in detail in the Walk in the Light series book entitled *The Law and Grace*.

[44] See Leviticus 23:2, 4, 37, 44. The texts specifically detail YHWH describing them as "My Appointed Times."

The Appointed Times are essentially considered to be "rehearsals" and they are not only critical for understanding the past, but also the future. In fact, one cannot understand prophecy or the mysterious Book of Revelation without understanding the moadim. Through those Appointed Times, the Creator has actually provided the framework for restoring Creation.

3

Covenants

As we have already mentioned, there are certain myths diffused throughout time that actually veil the truth they are supposed to transmit. Most people believe that Adam and Eve were the first man and woman who were deceived by a snake, ate an apple and then expelled from the Garden of Eden. This is the G-rated version of the event with many incorrect details. Again, the truth can be discerned in the Hebrew texts, but translations and traditions have clouded that truth.

For instance, the name of the woman was not Eve but, rather, Hawah (𐤄𐤅𐤇). It is a Hebrew name that means: "life-giver." This may seem trivial to some, after all, what's so important about a Name? Well, for anyone who actually believes the Bible, names are very important. This has already been established with the information concerning the Name of YHWH. Since the Scriptures provide that *"there is no other Name under heaven given among men by which we must be saved,"*[45] I consider names to be extremely important.

The so-called "serpent" participating in the Garden event was actually called the "nachash" (𐤔𐤇𐤍) in Hebrew. The Hebrew word "nachash" means: "shining one" and it can allude to divination or placing a spell on someone.

The event in the Garden involved more than simply eating from the wrong tree although, interestingly, a violation concerning the dietary instructions was the first recorded transgression. It amazes me how many Christians completely disregard the dietary instructions provided by the Creator. They erroneously categorize them as legalism and

---

[45] Acts 4:12

many flippantly proclaim that the Creator does not care about what we eat.

If He did not care about what we eat He would not have given the instructions in the first place.[46] He actually cares about everything that we do. He gave us instructions concerning food to keep us set apart and there are many health benefits associated with following the dietary instructions.[47]

If we cannot even regulate what we eat, how can we control the other appetites and cravings that tempt our flesh? We are not talking about legalism, just simple self-control and obedience which seems to be a scarce commodity in modern Christian culture. The Commandments are intended to aid us in conquering the flesh so that we can live in the spirit.[48] Failure to understand this simple truth will ultimately lead a person down the path of destruction.

In the case of Adam and Hawah, their sin involved a failure to obey the Commandments and to maintain distinctions. Both the man and the woman crossed the boundaries established for them. They profaned the image of the Creator by their actions. They failed to distinguish between clean and unclean - righteous conduct and the profane. These distinctions are critical for anyone who desires to dwell in the presence of a Holy (set apart) Elohim. The ultimate goal of "the satan"[49] is to delude and distract mankind to forget his high standing in creation and ignore those distinctions.

The enemy of mankind wants all men and women to exist and remain in a fallen and depraved state because that is

---

[46] It is important to distinguish between the very simple dietary instructions contained in the Scriptures as opposed to the very complex traditions of kashrut developed by the religion of Judaism.

[47] This subject is discussed in the Walk in the Light series book entitled *Kosher*.

[48] The Messiah taught the Commandments in the flesh as foundational, having a deeper spiritual application. See Matthew 5:21 – 48.

[49] The word "satan" is often used as a name, but it is actually a title. It comes from the Hebrew word "shatan" and it means: "adversary." In the Scriptures we often read about "ha'shatan" or "the satan" which literally means: "the adversary."

his fate. He rebelled against YHWH along with other fallen angels, known as the Nephilim.[50] At the heart of the matter is defiance toward YHWH and disobedience to the Commandments.

When Adam was placed in the Garden he was given specific instructions. He was told to *"tend and keep it."*[51] The word translated as "keep" is "shamar" (ٲﻤﻮ) in Hebrew. It means: "to guard and protect." Adam was charged with working and guarding this particular place on Earth where YHWH would come and fellowship with him. It was like the capital of the Kingdom of YHWH on Earth, a fortress that needed to be defended.[52]

Adam was supposed to represent the interests of YHWH. He was the first watchman commissioned by YHWH, but he failed to properly warn Hawah and protect the Garden from the deception perpetrated by the nachash. As a result, the man and the woman were seduced and defiled.

Because of their actions they could no longer dwell in the presence of a Holy Elohim. They deserved death, but were shown mercy. It is important to note that their actions were specifically tied to the Commandments. This is a fundamental principle ignored by many who have been seduced to believe that "grace" somehow negates the need to conduct ourselves in a righteous, set apart, manner. While grace is the means to deliver us from sin, many essentially treat grace as a license to sin.

---

[50] The Scriptures provide the following account: *"There were giants (Nephillim) on the earth in those days, and also afterward, when the sons of God came in to the daughters of men and they bore children to them. Those were the mighty men who were of old, men of renown."* Genesis 6:4. The Hebrew word "nephillim" is often transalted as "giants," but is better translated as "fallen ones." The fallen angels (nephillim), also known as Watchers, mated with the daughters of men and had offspring who became the mighty ones of reknown. In other words, those children of the fallen angels became the "demi-gods" of mythology with the "fallen angels" as the gods. They built their own kingdom and religion in direct opposition to the Kingdom of Elohim.

[51] Genesis 2:15

[52] The Hebrew word for "garden" is "gan" (ﻥﺝ) and it specifically refers to an enclosed, or protected space.

Their actions still had consequences. They were separated from Elohim but not killed. Blood was nevertheless required to be shed to atone for their actions, although that blood would not be their own. Instead of experiencing death, the man and the woman received grace through the blood of atonement. Innocent blood was shed at the threshold of the Garden on their behalf as they were provided coats of animal skin to cover their nakedness.

The word "atonement" is "kippur" (רפכ) in Hebrew, and it actually means: "covering." YHWH was revealing that He would some day provide atonement so that mankind could return to the House. This is an important event that is actually rehearsed every year through the Appointed Time of Yom Kippur.[53] Sadly, most have labeled this day a "Jewish Holiday" when, in fact, it is a day of prayer and fasting that is important for the entire world.[54]

The sin in the Garden involved prohibited interaction between mankind and angelic entities. What happened in the Garden was the beginning of the genetic corruption that was perpetrated upon mankind and all of creation. This cross breeding defiled the species distinctions established by YHWH.[55] It eventually led to the existence of giants and all sorts of hybrid beings that can only be described as monsters.

This is well documented in ancient texts and myths, but it does not fit well within the modern religious construct that is currently struggling to maintain its legitimacy amidst the veritable onslaught from the scientific arena. Sadly, instead of strictly interpreting the Scriptures modern Christianity often attempts to conform to science. To promote the actual accounts described in the Scriptures would likely be considered far-fetched and the stuff of

---

[53] See Leviticus 16
[54] Yom Kippur and it's significance to all mankind is discussed in the Walk in the Light series book entitled *Appointed Times*. It is also extremely pertinent when considering the final judgment at the end of the age. That is a subject discussed in the Walk in the Light series entitled *The Final Shofar*.
[55] Genesis 1:11, 1:21, 1:24

science fiction to the rational thinkers of the modern era.

As a result, we now see certain groups attempting to ascribe alien origins to those events that are actually well documented and easily explained in the Scriptures once we get past certain translation issues. There are also various other texts that support the Scriptural account.

The earth was flooded because of the corruption that eventually infected all flesh.[56] Noah and his family were not corrupted. In fact, in the Hebrew text we read that he was "tamayim" (𐤉𐤌𐤕𐤀) which means: "undefiled."[57] He also "walked" with Elohim. That means that he lived his life on the "righteous path" by following the Commandments of YHWH. Obedience to the Commandments is, after all, the very definition of righteousness.[58]

After the flood, Noah and his family repopulated the earth. It did not take long for mankind to, once again, rebel against YHWH. The Scriptures clearly describe that the Nephilim were before and after the flood.[59] There came a time when Nimrod established a government and a religious system directly opposed to YHWH. The Tower of Babel was the epitome of mankind's rebellion against YHWH. As a result, the languages were confused and the people were divided into the nations. Despite the diversity of languages, the people continued their rebellion and perpetrated their false religion throughout the planet.

Babylon was the source of sun worship that incorporated the worship of the fallen angels and their offspring as gods and demi-gods. This practice has continued through the ages. Amazingly, the people of the earth continue

---

[56] "So Elohim looked upon the earth, and indeed it was corrupt; for all flesh had corrupted their way on the earth." Genesis 6:12.

[57] Genesis 6:9 provides: "This is the genealogy of Noah. Noah was a just man, perfect in his generations. Noah walked with Elohim."

[58] Deuteronomy 6:17-25. It is important to note that simply following the Commandments will not repair the separation between mankind and Elohim created by the sin in the Garden. We must receive atonement by the blood of a perfect sacrifice that only YHWH can provide. Once we receive that atonement and are washed clean we are expected to follow the path of righteousness set forth in the Torah.

[59] Genesis 6:4

to participate in the same idolatrous practices that derive from Babylon, such as Christmas and Easter. The evidence is irrefutable but even when confronted with this truth, many shrug and state: "That's not what it means to me." They erroneously think that they can participate in pagan practices as long as they do it for YHWH. This is a serious mistake.

YHWH explains in His Torah how He desires to be worshiped. He specifically commands His people not to worship Him as the pagans worship their gods.[60] This is particularly egregious when Christians choose pagan times over the Appointed Times of YHWH. These are rooted in Babylonian sun worship and that is why YHWH exhorts His people to come out of Babylon.[61]

There was actually a pattern for exiting Babylon established and demonstrated through the life of a man named Abram. Abram was uncircumcised when He was called by YHWH. This is a condition likened to the nations of the world that were disbursed from Babylon after the Tower of Babel event.

Abram believed the promise of YHWH and he acted. In fact, his actions defined his relationship with YHWH and were the proof of his belief. That belief, demonstrated by his actions, was accounted to him as righteousness.[62] He crossed over into the Promised Land. This is the source of the word "Hebrew." It is "eber" (ⴳⵀⵔ) in the Hebrew language and it means: "to cross over."

The word "Hebrew" refers to all those who believe the promises of YHWH, exit Babylon by "crossing over through the waters of immersion" and inherit the Promised Land through a Covenant relationship.[63] That Covenant was

---

[60] Deuteronomy 12:30-31
[61] Revelation 18:4
[62] Genesis 15:6
[63] There were no bridges in those days. If you wanted to cross over a river it involved getting wet. This is why those who enter into the Covenant get baptized, or immersed. We get cleansed in preparation for our dwelling with a "holy" Elohim. It is symbolic of the complete cleansing that we receive when we are washed by the blood of the Lamb of Elohim.

the path that YHWH established for mankind to return to Him.

The Land represented a restoration to the Garden of Eden, only this time it would be populated by a group of people brought out of Babylon who were committed to obeying the Commandments of Elohim. These people would enter into a Covenant of Marriage with YHWH.

After leaving Babylon, the uncircumcised Abram entered into a Covenant relationship with YHWH. Through that Covenant, YHWH demonstrated that He would provide the "atonement" and incur the penalty for breaking the Covenant.[64] Through this Covenant, Abram was promised a great number of descendants and land for those descendants. This would be the path of restoration for mankind. The only way that mankind could dwell with YHWH was through a process of cleansing and restoring him to righteousness.

Later when he progressed into the Covenant of Circumcision Abram received the new name Abraham. His wife Sarai also received the new name Sarah. They both had the letter "hey" (ᕼ) added to their original names. The Hebrew letter "hey" (ᕼ) often represents the "breath or the spirit" and adding a "hey" (ᕼ) to these two individuals represents the fact that the Covenant involves being transformed by the Spirit of YHWH.[65]

The point of that Covenant was to reveal that the Kingdom would be established through the seed of Abraham - renewed beings circumcised in the flesh and in the hearts and filled with the Spirit of Elohim. This was a family affair and anyone was welcome to join into the Covenant. By entering into the Covenant, they joined the Covenant family.

---

[64] Genesis 15

[65] It is important to recall that the Name of YHWH (ᕼᎧᕼᎧ) in Hebrew includes two "heys" (ᕼ) joined together by a "vav" (Ꭹ). The vav is the sixth letter in the Hebrew alephbet and represents man. Recall that the "vav" (Ꭹ) was affixed to the aleph taw (ᚷᚷ) as the sixth word in the Scriptures, essentially connecting "the heavens" (ᛗᎧᛗᎧᕼ) and "the earth" (ᚱᎧᚷᕼ).

That Covenant extended through the descendants of Abraham, Isaac and the 12 sons of Jacob, who was renamed Israel. The 12 tribes eventually grew into a nation while enslaved in Egypt. Known collectively as the Children of Israel they were delivered from Egypt in a miraculous fashion so that the world would know the Name of YHWH.[66]

They were delivered along with a mixed multitude of people.[67] The point was clear that YHWH wanted the Nations to join into His Covenant through the Covenant established with Israel. In fact, He specifically stated that there was one Torah for the native Israelite and all the strangers who dwelled with them.[68]

This is a concept lost in time as the nation of Israel fragmented and divided into two separate kingdoms. Here is where it becomes important to understand history. To begin, the word Israel is more accurately rendered as "Yisrael" (𐤋𐤀𐤓𐤔𐤉). It is often translated as "He has striven with El."[69] We know the word "El" (𐤋𐤀) refers to Elohim, and what many have failed to recognize is that at the heart of the word Yisrael is "sar" (𐤓𐤔), which means: "prince" or "royalty."[70] So these people were meant to be a royal

---

[66] Exodus 9:16
[67] Exodus 12:38
[68] Exodus 12:49; Numbers 15:16
[69] This translation is based upon the event where Jacob wrestled with a "Man" until the break of day. The "Man" did not prevail and stated: "Your name shall no longer be called Jacob, but 𐤋𐤀𐤓𐤔𐤉-Yisrael; for you have struggled with 𐤉𐤅𐤋𐤀-Elohim and with 𐤉𐤅𐤔-men, and have prevailed." Genesis 32:28. There is an amazing word play found in the Hebrew text and I have provided some of those mysteries in the translated text. The word "em" (𐤉𐤅𐤀) means: "mother" while the word "am" (𐤉𐤅𐤔) means: "people or assembly." So while Jacob's name was being changed, we can see that this Yisrael would be the womb that would give birth to an Assembly of men who would be an assembly of Elohim.
[70] This fact was clearly revealed when YHWH stated: "And you shall be to Me a kingdom of priests and a holy nation. These are the words which you shall speak to the children of Yisrael." Exodus 19:6. This was the heart of the Covenant made with Abram and Sarai when their names were changed to Abraham and Sarah. "I will make you exceedingly fruitful; and I will make nations of you, and kings shall come from you." Genesis 17:6. "And I will bless her and also give you a son by her; then I will bless her, and she shall be a mother of nations; kings of peoples shall be from her." Genesis 17:16. This was later confirmed to the man newly named Yisrael. "¹⁰ And Elohim said to him, 'Your name is Jacob; your name shall not be called Jacob anymore, but Yisrael shall be your name.' So He called his name Yisrael. ¹¹ Also Elohim said to him: 'I am Elohim

assembly brought into relationship with YHWH through the Covenant.

In fact, after being brought out of Egypt, these people participated in a Marriage Covenant with YHWH at Mount Sinai. This group, collectively called Yisrael, became the Bride of YHWH. They were given the Torah as a "ketubah" (ﾖﾁﾔﾗﾕ), also known as a marriage contract. It set forth the terms of the relationship.

Yisrael was supposed to move into the marital residence, which was the Promised Land. Sadly, they feared the inhabitants of the Land, namely the giants, and refused to enter in. It is important to understand what was going on here. YHWH previously wiped out the children of the Nephilim through a flood. The Nephilim continued their corruption of creation and actually littered the Promised Land with their offspring, which were an abomination in the eyes of YHWH. Their DNA was mixed with the Nephilim which was a defilement of mankind - the image of Elohim.

This was a direct affront to YHWH and He intended to cleanse the Land with His new Bride, but she refused. He had already revealed His Mighty Hand by delivering her from bondage in Egypt, and was prepared to do the same as she entered into the Promised Land. Her response was a slap in the face to YHWH. After having previously broken the Covenant by committing idolatry with the Egyptian gods represented by the golden calf, Yisrael was once again betraying her Husband.

YHWH would therefore wait for the next generation to enter in. Under the leadership of Joshua, better known as Yahushua, Yisrael eventually entered in and took the Land.[71]

Almighty. *Be fruitful and multiply; a nation and a company of nations shall proceed from you, and kings shall come from your body.'"* Genesis 35:10-11.

[71] It is no coincidence that the leader who began as a servant of Mosheh and transformed into a conquering leader would be named Yahushua, the same name as the Messiah. This was a pattern that we would see fulfilled as he brought the Children of Yisrael across the Jordan as a corporate immersion and then circumcised them before he utterly destroyed the moon worshipping city of Jericho. This is a pattern that the Messiah will likely repeat in the future.

After hundreds of years YHWH gave Yisrael a King. The first king named Saul did not diligently obey the Commandments of YHWH. The reign was therefore removed from him and given to David, the son of Jesse. David first ruled over the House of Yahudah for seven years. He was later annointed by the House of Yisrael and ruled over a united kingdom for thirty-three years. He reigned forty years in all.

After the death of King David, his son Solomon assumed the throne. While Solomon is often remembered for the wisdom bestowed upon him, his life ended miserably. He violated the Torah and participated in the worst forms of idolatry. As a result, the Kingdom would be divided between the north and the south. For the sake of David, his offspring would retain a portion of the Kingdom known as the House of Judah.

The Covenant people were originally collectively called Yisrael, but after they were divided that name was attributed to the 10 tribes ruled by Ephraim.[72] They were called the House of Yisrael, or the Northern Kingdom. The remaining tribes were ruled by Judah, better known as Yahudah. These tribes were referred to as the House of Yahudah or the Southern Kingdom.

After separating, these two kingdoms individually rebelled and were exiled from the Promised Land. They both broke the Covenant and that Covenant needed to be restored with both Houses.

YHWH sent prophets to both Houses and promised a restoration. The House of Yahudah had been exiled by the Babylonians for 70 years, but only some returned at the end of the exile. She was never fully restored as a sovereign nation led by the seed of David. The House of Yisrael had been divorced, exiled by the Assyrians and scattered throughout the world. They needed a wedding in order to be restored to Him, and this was the context of and purpose of

---

[72] See 1 Kings 12:20

- 31 -

the Messiah. He would seek out the lost sheep of the House of Yisrael[73] and renew the Covenant with both Houses.[74]

[73] See Matthew 10:6 and 15:24 in the context of Jeremiah 50.
[74] Jeremiah 31:31-32

4

The Messiah

There are currently many people from diverse belief systems awaiting the return of a messiah. The expectations vary depending upon the particular religion. For instance, Muslims await al Mahdi to come and rule over an Islamic Caliphate. Jews are generally looking for a man to come and unite the divided Houses and restore the Kingdom of Yisrael as David had once done.[75]

Christians believe that the Messiah has already come. They believe that He died, was resurrected and will return again to rule the planet. They claim that He fulfilled the prophecies found in the very same texts used by the Jews. The question then is why don't the Jews also believe that the Messiah came.

The answer to this question is not too difficult to understand with a proper knowledge of history. First, it is important to point out that the Christian religion and popular historical renderings have done a remarkable job of hiding the true identity of the Messiah. They have changed His Name from Yahushua to Jesus. His Name is actually the same name as the patriarch often referred to as Joshua.

Those who refuse to use the proper Hebrew Name of the Messiah and insist upon calling Him by an English name are not being intellectually honest. The reason is that the English equivalent to Yahushua is Joshua, not Jesus. Now I am not encouraging people to call the Messiah Joshua, because I do not believe that names should change from one

---

[75] King David actually united the Tribes of Yisrael. He first ruled over the House of Yahudah for seven years and then was anointed by the House of Yisrael. Once he united all of the Tribes he moved the Capital from Hebron to Jerusalem. This was a pattern for the Messiah.

language to another. They may be transliterated, but they should always sound the same.

Again, remember that English is a relatively fledgling language, historically speaking. The letter "J" is an advent of the English language and did not exist in any of the ancient languages such as Hebrew, Aramaic, Greek or Latin. Therefore it is philologically impossible for the name of the Hebrew Messiah from the Tribe of Yahudah to be named Jesus. The simple fact is that the Messiah was never called Jesus when He walked the Earth. His Name was not, is not nor ever will be Jesus. It was and remains Yahushua and if you refuse to recognize this irrefutable historical fact then you are ironically committing the same sin as the Pharisees. You have chosen a tradition over truth and your choice is a direct affront to the Messiah.

It is not just the letter "J" that is the problem. There is also no etymological connection between the English name Jesus and the Hebrew name Yahushua. In fact, the name Jesus derives from the Greek Iesus, which is directly related to a mythological child of Zeus.[76] What we see in the Christian representation of the Messiah is more blending of pagan sun worship and that is a difficult thing for most Jews to get past. To them, Christianity is very much a pagan religion. Sadly, the Name of the Messiah is not the only Babylonian influence that exists in the Christian religion.

As mentioned previously, the Christian religion celebrates the birth of the Messiah on Christmas, which is a

---

[76] Iesus was actually a healing deity, so it is not difficult to understand how the Messiah could get tagged with this name. Especially when one recognizes that the original faith in the Messiah grew in ranks by incorporating converted pagans. These pagans often came loaded with certain "baggage" and ended up blending their pagan practices and ideas with their newly found faith. This is how the Gnostics became so prevalent early on. The Greek New Testament manuscripts actually replace the name of Elijah with Helios, a pagan sun god. This is because they both had stories relating to riding a chariot into the heavens. As a result, the pagans replaced an unfamiliar Hebrew name with a familiar pagan name. This is not proper, but it was done. The Roman Catholic Church has a well established history of adopting and transforming the customs of their pagan converts, and blending them into their traditions. This practice is known as "syncretism." So things have been altered and changed to suit the needs of converts. Regrettably, this is an undeniable fact. The subject is discussed further in the Walk in the Light series books entitled *Restoration* and *Names*.

Babylonian derived tradition associated with the winter solstice. Most all sun worshippers around the world and through the ages believed that the sun god was born, or reborn, on December 25. Due to the procession of the equinoxes the winter solstice now falls on December 21, but at the time that the Babylonian traditions originated it was December 25. Yahushua, the Messiah of Yisrael, was actually born on an Appointed Time of YHWH.[77]

The Christian religion also celebrates the resurrection of the Messiah on Easter. Easter is the name of a Babylonian derived sun goddess and it is an annual pagan fertility celebration.[78] This is why rabbits and eggs remain part of the Easter traditions. They are fertility symbols.

Of course, the inclusion of Babylonian sun worship within the religion of Christianity should be no surprise to anyone who understands that the birth of Christianity traces directly to the Roman Empire, not the Messiah. The Roman Emperor Constantine was a sun worshiper, and the creation of Christianity was a political solution to save his fractured and eroding empire. It is important to remember that the empire that created this religion is the same empire that killed the Messiah.

The Christian religion instituted by the Roman Empire was very different from the Covenant faith of Yisrael lived and taught by the Messiah. In fact, it was a counterfeit religion that quickly separated from the Covenant faith of YHWH found in the Torah. It is actually opposed to the commandments of YHWH set forth in the Torah. That is why most Christians are directed away from the Torah. They call it the "Old Testament" and most do not feel that they should obey the righteous Commandments of YHWH

---

[77] The Messiah was born on the Appointed Time known as Yom Teruah, the Day of Blasting, sometimes called Rosh HaShanah which means: "the head of the year." This memorializes Day 1 of Creation when the light was caused to shine in the darkness. The birth of Yahushua is discussed in detail in the Walk in the Light series book entitled *The Messiah*.

[78] The incorporation of pagan celebrations into the religion of Christianity is discussed in the Walk in the Light series books entitled *Restoration* and *Pagan Holidays*.

found in the Torah. This is a fundamental tenet of Christianity espoused through the notion of "grace."[79]

The Christian religion has also seriously misrepresented the teachings of Yahushua. He came preaching repentance, which involved a return to YHWH and His Commandments.[80] During one of His first recorded teachings He proclaimed:

"[17] Do not think that I came to destroy the Torah or the Prophets. I did not come to destroy but to fulfill. [18] For assuredly, I say to you, till heaven and earth pass away, one jot or one tittle will by no means pass from the Torah till all is fulfilled. [19] Whoever therefore breaks one of the least of these Commandments, and teaches men so, shall be called least in the Kingdom of Heaven; but whoever does and teaches them, he shall be called great in the Kingdom of Heaven. [20] For I say to you, that unless your righteousness exceeds the righteousness of the scribes and Pharisees, you will by no means enter the Kingdom of Heaven." Matthew 5:17-20.

Notice that Yahushua specifically stated that He did not come to destroy the Torah, but that is exactly what many teach that He did. To the contrary, He came to fulfill the Torah by living it as YHWH intended. As the Word of Elohim, He provided the example. You see the Pharisees had disobeyed the express commandment not to add to or take away from the Torah.[81]

They had added to and taken away from the Torah by their traditions, which were treated as if they were "Law." They were promoting and teaching their own traditions as

---

[79] Most Christians are taught, and generally believe, that the Messiah did away with the Torah through "grace." This is contrary to the express statement of Messiah when He stated: *"[17] Do not think that I came to destroy the Torah or the Prophets. I did not come to destroy but to fulfill. [18] For assuredly, I say to you, till heaven and earth pass away, one jot or one tittle will by no means pass from the law till all is fulfilled."* Matthew 5:17-18. His fulfillment of the Torah and the Prophets has nothing to do with destroying or doing away with them. The Torah and the Prophets exist and are relevant until heaven and earth pass away, whenever that is. We can state for certain that that time has not yet arrived. This subject is discussed in detail in the Walk in the Light series book entitled *The Law and Grace*.
[80] Matthew 4:17
[81] Deuteronomy 4:2, 12:32

being equal or above the Commandments of YHWH. This was the issue at the heart of much of the controversy that Yahushua had with them.[82] That is why He proclaimed that your righteousness must <u>exceed</u> that of the Pharisees. They were deriving their righteousness from their traditions. As a result, they are not getting into the Kingdom. True righteousness is found in the Torah just as Yahushua taught and lived.

While many of the Jews believed Yahushua and followed Him, the Pharisees, as a separate sect of Yisrael, opposed Him. After the destruction of the Temple in 70 CE, the Pharisees became the predominate sect of Yisraelites apart from the followers of Yahushua, who were sometimes called Natzrenes.

This is where history and division take over. Each sect essentially formed a new religion, separate and apart from the original faith of Yahushua and the Covenant path that YHWH established for Yisrael. The Pharisees ended up establishing the religion of Judaism. The Natzrenes ended up becoming overrun with Gentiles who diluted the faith until the Roman Empire developed the religion of Christianity. Christianity originated as a blending of the Natzrene faith and sun worship.

Christianity, as we see it today, does not represent the walk that Yahushua taught. It claims a separate and distinct identity from Yisrael, which has no basis in the Scriptures. Remember that the Covenant flowed from Abram to Yisrael. Yisrael always represented the Covenant people of YHWH. Just because they broke the Covenant does not mean that YHWH is finished with them. In fact, it was specifically revealed that YHWH, through His Son, would bear the

---

[82] A good example of the controversy between Yahushua and the Pharisees can be seen in Mark 7. The Pharisees were criticizing Yahushua and His disciples for not following the tradition concerning the washing of hands. Yahushua rebuked them for rejecting the commandments and holding to their traditions. They had essentially elevated their traditions over the simple commandments of YHWH.

punishment for their breaking the Covenant.[83]

Yisrael, after all, was the Bride of YHWH. While she was divided and punished, the prophecies promised a regathering and reuniting through the Messiah. Here is one of many prophecies attesting to that fact. "[21] *Then say to them, Thus says the Master YHWH: 'Surely I will take the children of Yisrael from among the nations, wherever they have gone, and will gather them from every side and bring them into their own land;* [22] *and I will make them one nation in the land, on the mountains of Yisrael; and one king shall be king over them all; they shall no longer be two nations, nor shall they ever be divided into two kingdoms again.* [23] *They shall not defile themselves anymore with their idols, nor with their detestable things, nor with any of their transgressions; but I will deliver them from all their dwelling places in which they have sinned, and will cleanse them. Then they shall be My people, and I will be their Elohim.*" Ezekiel 37:21-23.[84]

The Messiah came to renew the Covenant with Yisrael. He did not come to establish a new and different covenant with some fictitious entity called the Church. The word "church" is actually another English word that has been inserted into English translations and developed into a tradition contravening the actual content of the New Testament texts.

That simple translation issue entirely distorts and misrepresents the plan of YHWH. The use of this word supports the popular teaching in Christianity that YHWH is finished with Yisrael and leads many people to believe that the church is something new in the plan of YHWH. This is because the word "church" only appears in the New Testament and not in the Old Testament.

What people need to understand is that the Greek word "ekklesia" (ἐκκλησία) that is often translated as "church" means the same thing as the Hebrew word "qahal"

---

[83] See Genesis 15 and 22

[84] For a detailed discussion of the prophecies concerning the re-gathering and reuniting of the divided kingdom see the Walk in the Light series books entitled *The Redeemed* and *The Final Shofar*.

(𐤋𐤒𐤄𐤟) that frequently is used to refer to the "assembly" of Yisrael in the Old Testament. Therefore, in the New Testament when we read about the "ekklesia" we should be directed to the "qahal" which is the Covenant "assembly" of Yisrael – not some new group of people called the church consisting of Christians.

This notion is mind boggling for most Christians who have been taught that Jesus did away with the Torah and started a new religion called Christianity that revolves around a new group of people called The Church. That is a foundational tenet of Christian doctrine, but it is simply not supported by the Scriptures when viewed in their original context and language.

Now if you are a Christian and feel defensive by this message do not fret. You need to step back, take a deep breath and relax. This book is not about attacking the faith of Yahushua, rather it is all about restoring the truth of His message. That message may be different from what you have been taught, but the Scriptures confirm everything contained in this discussion. Therefore, all you need to do is test whether your beliefs derive from the Scriptures or from tradition.

The simple truth is that Yahushua came exactly as the prophecies foretold. He fulfilled the Torah by showing us the way of the Torah that leads us back to the House. He opened the door for anyone to enter into the Covenant. Through the Passover, His blood was sprinkled at the threshold of the house as demonstrated by the pattern of the Garden. His blood provided atonement on the doorpost so will pass over us and we can have life.

That is the "amazing grace" mentioned in the beginning that we sing about in the famous hymn. It is the free gift afforded to everyone. We cannot earn that gift. The question then is what do we do with that gift? Once we have been made clean by the blood of the Lamb, do we continue to walk in the filth of disobedience or do we walk in the light of

His Commandments?

Yahushua gave a clear and unequivocal answer. He said: *"If you love Me, keep My Commands."* John 14:15. This was the same instruction given to Adam and Yisrael. The word translated as "keep" is "shamar" (ᐊᵞШ) in Hebrew. Again, it means to "watch, guard and protect."

The night before His crucifixion, Yahushua participated in the Covenant meal of the Passover. It was during this meal that He began the renewal of the Covenant with Yisrael as the High Priest according to the Order of Melchizedek.[85] He stated that the bread represented His body and the wine represented His blood.[86] His presence at the Passover meal represented the Passover Lamb – the Lamb of Elohim. Later, on Passover Day, His body would be broken and His blood would be shed just as had been symbolically done with the bread and the wine at the Passover meal.

How interesting that there were 12 disciples at that Covenant meal, representing the 12 tribes of Yisrael. One of them left before the meal was completed. His name was Judas, which means Judah, or rather Yahudah. It was during this Appointed Time that the Covenant was renewed.

It was not a brand new Covenant, but rather the long anticipated renewal promised by the prophets. The renewal would be with the House of Yisrael and the House of Yahudah.[87] There is no Covenant prophesied with an entity called the Church. *"But this is the Covenant that I will make with the House of Yisrael after those days, says YHWH: I will put My Torah in their minds, and write it on their hearts; and I will be their Elohim, and they shall be My people."* Jeremiah 31:33.

This is critical to understand because your future depends upon your relationship with YHWH and His Son. That relationship is defined by a Covenant. You must determine whether or not you are in that Covenant before it

---

[85] See Genesis 14:18, Psalm 110:1-4, Hebrews 5-7
[86] Matthew 26:26-29, Mark 14:22-25, Luke 22:19-22
[87] Jeremiah 31:31-34

is too late. Many will in fact be deceived and will be rejected by the Messiah. They will think that they are in a relationship with the Son, but they will be wrong.

Here is a very chilling statement made by Yahushua. *"²¹ Not everyone who says to Me, Lord, Lord, shall enter the Kingdom of Heaven, but he who does the will of My Father in heaven. ²² Many will say to Me in that day, 'Lord, Lord, have we not prophesied in Your name, cast out demons in Your name, and done many wonders in Your name?' ²³ And then I will declare to them, 'I never knew you; depart from Me, you who practice lawlessness!'"* Matthew 7:21-23.

Notice that there will be <u>many</u> people calling Him "Lord." They think that they are following Him and doing His will but they are actually deceived. He does not know them, which means He does not have a relationship with them. They may be running around doing all sorts of seemingly religious activities, but they are not in Covenant with Him. He actually defines them by their actions - they are "lawless." The Greek word is "anomia" (ἀνομία), which specifically means: "without the Torah."

Only those who do "the will of the Father" will enter into the Kingdom and "the will of the Father" is expressed through the Commandments. The Christian religion is notorious for rejecting the Torah and claiming their "liberty" through "grace." They misunderstand both the Torah and grace, and the writings of Paul are often used to justify a rejection of the Torah because of that grace.[88]

Those who subscribe to such false teachings do so to their own destruction. They should expect to be sent away by Yahushua. He shed His blood so that you can be forgiven, cleansed and restored to the Renewed Covenant. If you reject the very Covenant that was offered to you by grace, then your fate has been determined.

Yahushua clearly stated who would inherit the

---

[88] The relationship between the Torah and grace is examined in detail in the Walk in the Light series book entitled *The Law and Grace*.

kingdom – "the poor in spirit."[89] "To be poor in spirit means to have emptied yourself of all desire to exercise personal self-will, and, what is just as important, to have renounced all preconceived opinions in the wholehearted search for [Elohim]. It means to be willing to set aside your present habits of thought, your present views and prejudices, your present way of life if necessary; to jettison, in fact, anything and everything that can stand in the way of your finding [Elohim]."[90] This includes any inherited customs and traditions that do not conform to the Scriptures.

There is a wedding feast being prepared by the Messiah and all are invited. You must make yourself ready and come on His terms, not your own terms. Those who refuse to do it His way will find themselves cast into outer darkness where there will be weeping and gnashing of teeth.[91]

---

[89] Matthew 5:3
[90] *The Sermon on the Mount, The Key to Success in Life,* Emmet Fox, Grosset & Dunlap (1938) page 22.
[91] Matthew 22:1-14

5

In the End

As we approach the end of the age many Christians eagerly anticipate the imminent return of the Messiah. Sadly, many are unprepared for His return because they fail to understand His true purpose and identity as revealed through the Hebrew Scriptures, language, culture and history. Those steeped in modern Christianity have inherited certain western traditions concerning His Name, His teachings and even His appearance that are historically inaccurate. Tradition has, once again, taken precedence over truth.

As a result, the expectations of many concerning the future are erroneous and a paradigm shift is required to distinguish truth from tradition. Probably one of the simplest, yet profound, examples that impacted my perception involved an unassuming instrument called a "shofar" (𐤀𐤅𐤔).

The shofar is a "ram's horn." It is used as a warning device, a call to assemble, an instrument of praise, a battle cry and even a weapon. The shofar is sounded at certain Appointed Times and it also announces the Jubilee.[92] The sound of the shofar has even been likened to the voice of Elohim.[93] There are different sounding blasts associated with the shofar, each with its own unique purpose. The Book of Revelation indicates that there will be seven shofar blasts at the end of the age announcing the return of the Messiah.[94] Incredibly, I never even heard or read the word "shofar" until

---

[92] See Jeremiah 6:1, 6:17, 4:5, 51:27; Ezekiel 33:3-6; Exodus 19:13; Psalm 150:3; Joshua 6; Judges 7; Nehemiah 4; Psalm 81:3; Leviticus 25:9. These passages are only a sampling of the passages involving the "shofar" that are typically translated as "trumpet" in English translations.
[93] See Exodus 19-20; Revelation 1:10
[94] Revelation 8-11

I traveled to the modern State of Israel.[95]

The translation of the Scriptures that I read my entire life never included the word shofar. Instead, they replaced the Hebrew word "shofar" with the English word "trumpet." Now these are two distinctly different sound emitting devices with unique functions. The Scriptures actually describe specific times when the shofar is blasted and there are specific times when the trumpet is sounded. Knowing this information can have incredible implications in the future, particularly when examining the seven shofar blasts in Revelation. A failure to recognize this very simple translation issue can have a profound impact on a person's fate.

This was shocking to me and when I recognized the enormity of this issue it started me on a quest to discover what else had been hidden from me. From this very brief examination it should be apparent that there is incredible truth located within the Scriptures that is being lost in translation and through traditions.

As we saw from the beginning, the message contained in the Scriptures is about YHWH building a House and filling that House with a Covenant family. After the fall and expulsion from the Garden, the door to the House was slammed shut.

YHWH sent His Son to die as the Lamb of Elohim. His blood on the mantel of the door would make the way for mankind to reenter the House. That is why He stated: *"I am the door."*[96] He also stated: *"Behold I stand at the door and knock. If anyone hears My voice and opens the door, I will come in to him and eat with him, and he with Me."*[97] This is all about a

---

[95] The modern State of Israel is not to be confused with the Covenant Assembly (qahal) of Yisrael. While the modern State of Israel likely consists of the physical decendants of the House of Yahudah, it is not currently observing the Torah and it does not recognize that the House of Yisrael must be restored and returned and both Houses must be united under the Messiah in order for the prophecies to be fulfilled. This will be the context of the end of the age. This subject is discussed in greater detail in the Walk in the Light series books entitled *The Redeemed* and *The Final Shofar*.

[96] John 10:7, 9

[97] Revelation 3:20

Covenant and a Covenant is sealed with a meal.

The Covenant begins at the door and is consummated through a meal, which includes the shed the blood of the covenant. This is the point of the Passover. It was a traditional blood covenant ritual that began at the threshold of the Yisraelite houses in Egypt and continued to the House of YHWH in the Promised Land. But as we can discern from the progression of the Appointed Times through the year, it was only the beginning.[98] Mankind needs to be cleansed and renewed. They need to have hearts to obey. Simply put, they need to have their hearts circumcised. This was always the purpose of the Torah.[99] If you want to live in the House, you need to learn the rules of the House. If you ignore those rules then you will not be permitted in the House. It is really that simple.

Those who believe that they can receive the grace of Elohim, be cleansed by the blood of Messiah and then live lives of sin and lawlessness are sadly mistaken. In fact, this will result in punishment of the highest order rendered upon those who have *"trampled the Son of Elohim underfoot, counted the blood of the Covenant by which He was sanctified a common thing, and insulted the Spirit of grace."*[100]

This is just as true in the end as it was in the beginning. YHWH does not change.[101] He has declared the end from the very beginning. Hear the words of YHWH spoken through the Prophet Isaiah:

---

[98] The Appointed Times are mentioned throughout the Torah, but the primary passage is found in Leviticus 23. It is there that we see the Appointed Times described by YHWH as "My Appointed Times." We also see the Covenant path laid out through these yearly rehearsals. It begins with the Passover meal, followed by a seven day Feast called the Feast of Unleavened Bread. After 50 days the Feast of Shabuot is celebrated, which is the culmination of the grain harvest. Also known as "firstfruits," it is the time when people bring their firstfruits from all over the Land to the House of YHWH. Then in the Seventh Month there is the Feast of Trumpets, followed by Yom Kippur, Succot and Shemini Atzeret. These all have a specific purpose and lead the Covenant people on the path to restoration. For a more detailed discussion of the Appointed Times see the Walk in the Light series book entitled *Appointed Times*.

[99] See Deuteronomy 10:16, 30:6, Jeremiah 4:4 and Ezekiel 36:26

[100] Hebrews 10:29

[101] Malachi 3:6

"9 Remember the former things of old, for I am Elohim, and there is no other; I am Elohim, and there is none like Me, 10 Declaring the end from the beginning, and from ancient times things that are not yet done, Saying, 'My counsel shall stand, and I will do all My pleasure,' 11 Calling a bird of prey from the east, the man who executes My counsel, from a far country. Indeed I have spoken it; I will also bring it to pass. I have purposed it; I will also do it. 12 Listen to Me, you stubborn-hearted, who are far from righteousness: 13 I bring My righteousness near, it shall not be far off; My salvation shall not linger. And I will place salvation in Zion, for Yisrael My glory." Isaiah 46:9-13.

Just as we saw the Messiah in the beginning, the Word, represented by the Aleph Taw (✗✗), we also see Him in the end. There is a perfect continuity and flow in the Scriptures that is only understood when viewed from a Hebraic perspective. Yisrael is the glory of YHWH and Yisrael will be the bride in the end.[102]

In fact, due to translation issues many people miss the connection specifically made by Yahushua. In the mysterious Book of Revelation, most English translations describe Yahushua as stating that He is "the Alpha and the Omega."[103] What they fail to recognize is that He is a Hebrew Messiah speaking to a Hebrew disciple. He would have been speaking in the Hebrew language.

Alpha (A) is the first letter in the Greek alphabet and Omega (Ω) is the last letter in the Greek alphabet. Since He was not speaking Greek, we understand that He did not refer

---

[102] Clearly, we are not talking about the Modern State of Israel, which does not currently recognize the Messiah or follow the Torah. While many citizens in the modern state may join in the Covenant and become part of the Yisrael of YHWH, the two are not the same. This has caused great confusion, especially involving the prophecies, as people attempt to apply the prophecies concerning the Covenant Assembly of Yisrael to the modern State of Israel.

[103] Revelation 1:8, 1:11, 21:6, 22:13

to Himself as the Alpha and the Omega (AΩ), but rather, the Aleph Taw (✗✗). So here we have a declaration from Yahushua that He is the Light and the Word from the beginning. He will come again in the end. Many will be unprepared for His coming because they have been taught lies and they do not know Him.

This was specifically revealed by Yahushua in the parable of the 10 virgins. *"¹ Then the kingdom of heaven shall be likened to ten virgins who took their lamps and went out to meet the bridegroom. ² Now five of them were wise, and five were foolish. ³ Those who were foolish took their lamps and took no oil with them, ⁴ but the wise took oil in their vessels with their lamps. ⁵ But while the bridegroom was delayed, they all slumbered and slept. ⁶ And at midnight a cry was heard: Behold, the bridegroom is coming; go out to meet him! ⁷ Then all those virgins arose and trimmed their lamps. ⁸ And the foolish said to the wise, Give us some of your oil, for our lamps are going out. ⁹ But the wise answered, saying, No, lest there should not be enough for us and you; but go rather to those who sell, and buy for yourselves. ¹⁰ And while they went to buy, the bridegroom came, and those who were ready went in with him to the wedding; and the door was shut. ¹¹ Afterward the other virgins came also, saying, Lord, Lord, open to us! ¹² But he answered and said, Assuredly, I say to you, I do not know you."* Matthew 25:1-12.

Notice that all 10 were virgins and wanted to be with the Bridegroom. Only 5 were considered wise while the remaining 5 were foolish. All fell asleep but the 5 wise were ready when the call was sounded. The foolish virgins were unprepared and ended up being shut out of the wedding feast. They did not properly discern the times and their lack of knowledge and preparedness had devastating consequences.

YHWH declared through the Prophet Hosea: *"My people are destroyed for lack of knowledge. Because you have rejected knowledge I also will reject you from being priest for Me. Because you have forgotten the Torah of your Elohim, I also will forget your children."* Hosea 4:6.

We are currently living in a time when many of the

called are sleeping. They lack knowledge and they have forgotten the Torah. They are unaware of the Appointed Times of YHWH and therefore they will be unprepared when the Messiah returns. As we approach the end of the age you must ask yourself whether you will be grouped with the wise or the foolish virgins? Will you be ready for the wedding feast or will you be shut out?

YHWH is in the process of restoring His people and preparing them for the promised great regathering. Just as the Children of Yisrael were separated, protected and delivered from the bondage of Egypt through the Appointed Times in the midst of judgment, the same is about to occur again, only on a global scale. In fact, this future deliverance will make the past exodus pale in comparison.[104] Just as the mixed multitude was gathered along with Yisrael, so will a Covenant people from all the nations be gathered to YHWH. This will occur at the end of the age when the nations are judged as described in the Book of Revelation.

This truth has been obscured and hidden due to religions and denominational factions interpreting the Scriptural texts to suit their own agenda. It is time for those who desire to know truth to shed the traditions of man that have been heaped upon them and begin to undergo restoration and a return to the ways of YHWH.

This book should not be viewed as an attack on any religion or denomination, but rather a call to restoration for those who are drawn to the voice of the Messiah and recognize that they have inherited lies. If you are a Christian and are feeling defensive that is only natural. The truths contained in this book may be shocking. In some instances they completely contradict the traditions that are being taught in mainstream Christianity.

It is a humbling experience to realize that you have been deceived to such an extent. It is also a real eye opener to recognize the degree of cunning and stealth exercised by the

---

[104] Jeremiah 16:14-15

adversary. The battle for the souls of mankind is raging while most are completely deluded to the extent of the deception and the reality of this existence. As they daily busy themselves with the cares of the world, they are being choked like seeds that fall among the thorns.[105] It certainly makes you appreciate the cleverness of the adversary. The same nachash that deceived Adam and Hawah continues his divination on mankind and he wants to destroy you through your religion.

The modern Christian religion clearly lacks the power demonstrated by the early Assembly because they fail to fully understand the Scriptures or the power of Elohim.[106] This is due to the fact that the Christian religion has generally rejected the standard of righteousness set forth in the Torah and has mixed with the pagan traditions of the world.

Christianity teaches that a person who obeys the righteous instructions of the Torah is legalistic. This creates an incredible paradox for Christians because the Torah is considered to be wisdom and understanding for the Covenant people. It is intended for the Bride, to set her apart from the nations and allow her to approach YHWH. It is supposed to be diligently obeyed by those in a Covenant relationship with YHWH.[107]

This has never changed and the Messiah came as a shepherd to gather His flock and restore them to the purity of the Torah through the Renewed Covenant. The early

---

[105] See Matthew 13, Mark 4 and Luke 8
[106] This was the same rendered upon the Pharisees by Yahushua who did not believe in the resurrection. See Matthew 22:29 and Mark 12:24.
[107] "5 Surely I have taught you statutes and judgments, just as YHWH my Elohim commanded me, that you should act according to them in the land which you go to possess. 6 Therefore be careful to observe them; for this is your wisdom and your understanding in the sight of the peoples who will hear all these statutes, and say, Surely this great nation is a wise and understanding people. 7 For what great nation is there that has Elohim so near to it, as YHWH our Elohim is to us, for whatever reason we may call upon Him? 8 And what great nation is there that has such statutes and righteous judgments as are in all this Torah which I set before you this day? 9 Only take heed to yourself, and diligently keep yourself, lest you forget the things your eyes have seen, and lest they depart from your heart all the days of your life. And teach them to your children and your grandchildren, 10 especially concerning the day you stood before YHWH your Elohim in Horeb, when YHWH said to me, Gather the people to Me, and I will let them hear My words, that they may learn to fear Me all the days they live on the earth, and that they may teach their children." Deuteronomy 4:5-10.

followers of Yahushua were Torah observant Yisraelites. They kept the Commandments of Elohim and they had the testimony of Yahushua. They were able to receive the infilling of the Holy Spirit more correctly called the Set Apart Spirit because they were set apart – qadosh. As a result, they could operate in the power of the Spirit. This will be the same characteristic of the true servants in the end as they return to the Commandments. They will also have the right to, once again, partake of the Tree of Life.[108]

This was why the disciples maintained the ritual of "baptism," better known as "immersion."[109] When a person repented, the immersion symbolized a cleansing from sin and a crossing over from death to life – from Babylon to Yisrael.

The point was to get clean by the blood of the Lamb of Elohim and then stop sinning. Entering into the Covenant meant joining the Kingdom of YHWH and the Torah is the constitution of that Kingdom. The Torah defines sin and reveals the righteous conduct that YHWH expects from us. As a result, after receiving salvation by grace, we need to follow the Torah and exercise righteous living. The Set Apart Spirit will not dwell in a defiled temple. The early Believers could readily receive the Set Apart Spirit because they understood the need to live righteously.[110]

In fact, the first major outpouring of the Spirit described in the Book of Acts occurred at the Appointed Time known as Shavuot.[111] Those who were in Jerusalem in

---

[108] Revelation 12:17, 14:12 and 22:14

[109] The immersion process was an integral part of meeting with YHWH at His House. All would immerse, which symbolized a cleansing from sin, before entering into His presence and doing business with Him.

[110] According to the Book of Acts, new converts were given certain preliminary Commandments to obey with the understanding that Moses (the Torah) was read in the Synagogues every Sabbath. (Acts 15:21). In other words, they were given certain immediate instructions to get them cleaned up from the defilements of the pagan lives that they were coming out of. (Acts 15:19-20). They were then expected to attend the Synagogue and learn the Torah each week. They could then continue to apply the righteous commandments to their lives as needed. This advice was deemed good by the elders and the Holy (Set Apart) Spirit. (Acts 15:28).

[111] Christianity calls this Appointed Time "Pentecost," but it is Shavuot in Hebrew – the Feast of Weeks. It is an important time after the grain harvest when the firstfruits are

obedience to the Commandments were in the right place at the right time to receive the message of the Good News in their own language as the Spirit gave utterance. It is no coincidence that this was the same Appointed Time when YHWH spoke the Commandments before the Set Apart Assembly at Mount Sinai centuries earlier. The relationship between the Torah and the Spirit is inseparable and those who worship YHWH must worship in Spirit and in Truth (Torah).[112]

If you have read up to this point it should be evident that you have been given a gift and an opportunity. Just as Yisrael was given the gift of the Torah, so too, the Messiah presents Himself, the Torah made flesh, to those who desire to be part of His Bride. Now it is time for you to decide whether you will choose the narrow way of the Covenant revealed by the Messiah or the broad way developed by the traditions of religions and men. Yahushua made it clear where each path leads.[113]

At the beginning of this book I promised that it would offer a life changing experience. Consider this your opportunity to begin the adventure of a lifetime. Every journey begins with the first step and yours begins by accepting this invitation - An Invitation to Walk in the Light!

gathered to the House of YHWH. It is a rehearsal intended to prepare those in Covenant with YHWH for the Great Harvest at the end of the age.
[112] John 4:23. The Torah is specifically defined as truth in Psalm 119:142.
[113] "Enter by the narrow gate; for wide is the gate and broad is the way that leads to destruction, and there are many who go in by it." Matthew 7:13.

The Walk in the Light Series

living.

Book 10	Appointed Times – Discusses the appointed times established by the Creator, often erroneously considered to be "Jewish" holidays, and critical to the understanding of prophetic fulfillment of the Scriptural promises.
Book 11	Pagan Holidays – Discusses the pagan origins of some popular Christian holidays which have replaced the Appointed Times.
Book 12	The Final Shofar – Examines the ancient history of the earth and prepares the Believer for the deceptions coming in the end of the age. Also discusses the walk required by the Scriptures to be an overcomer and endure to the end.

To order any of the books in the
Walk in the Light Series in print or ebook format
visit:

www.shemayisrael.net

The Shema

Deuteronomy (Debarim) 6:4-5

Traditional English Translation

Hear, O Israel: The LORD our God, the LORD is one!
You shall love the LORD your God with all your heart,
with all your soul, and with all your strength.

Corrected English Translation

Hear, O Yisrael: YHWH our Elohim, YHWH is one (unified)!
You shall love YHWH your Elohim with all your heart,
with all your soul, and with all your strength.

Modern Hebrew Text

שמע ישראל יהוה אלהינו יהוה אחד
ואהבת את יהוה אלהיך בכל־ לבבך ובכל־ נפשך ובכל־ מאדך

Ancient Hebrew Text

𐤔𐤌𐤏 𐤉𐤔𐤓𐤀𐤋 𐤉𐤄𐤅𐤄 𐤀𐤋𐤄𐤉𐤍𐤅 𐤉𐤄𐤅𐤄 𐤀𐤇𐤃
𐤅𐤀𐤄𐤁𐤕 𐤀𐤕 𐤉𐤄𐤅𐤄 𐤀𐤋𐤄𐤉𐤇 𐤁𐤊𐤋-𐤋𐤁𐤁𐤇
𐤅𐤁𐤊𐤋-𐤍𐤐𐤔𐤇 𐤅𐤁𐤊𐤋-𐤌𐤀𐤃𐤇

Hebrew Text Transliterated

Shema, Yisra'el: YHWH Elohenu, YHWH echad!
V-ahavta et YHWH Elohecha b-chol l'bacha u-b-chol
naf'sh'cha u-b-chol m'odecha.

The Shema has traditionally been one of the most important prayers in Judaism and has been declared the first (resheet) of all the Commandments. (Mark 12:29-30).